Evaluation of anti-microbial and anti-inflammatory action of castor and papaya seed extracts against *Staphylococcus aureus*

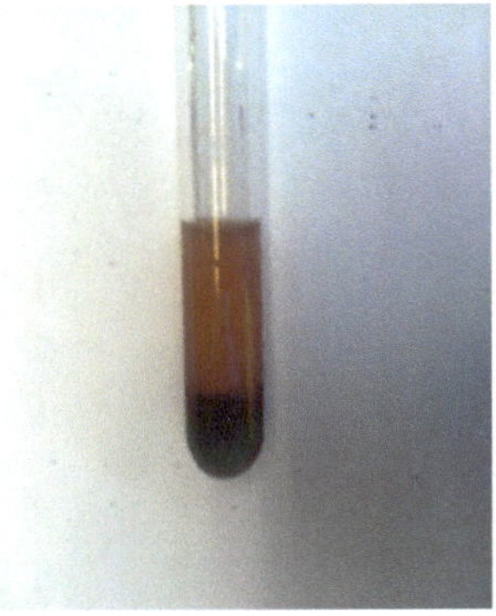

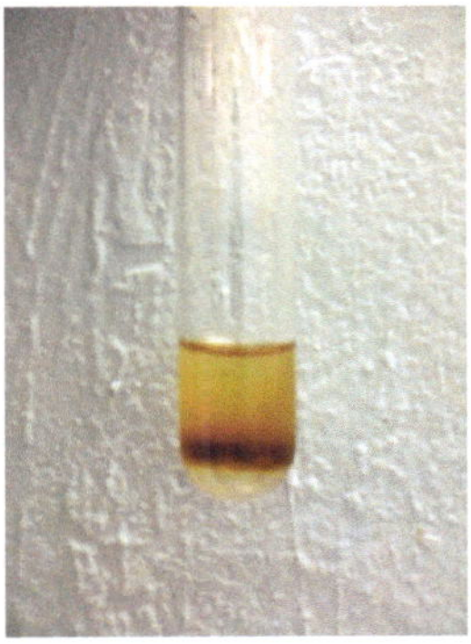

Prem Jose Vazhacharickal, John Joseph and Ravathy Krishna

Table of contents

Table of figures

Table of tables

List of abbreviations

μg	: Microgram
%	: Percentage
°C	: Degree celcius
C	: Control
C. papaya	: *Carica papaya*
g	: Gram
mg	: Milligram
ml	: Millilitre
mm	: Millimeter
nm	: Nanometer
OD	: Optical density
R. communis	: *Ricinus communis*
S. aureus	: *Staphylococcus aureus*
Sp	: Species
T	: Test
μl	: Microlitre

Evaluation of anti-microbial and anti-inflammatory action of castor and papaya seed extracts against *Staphylococcus aureus*

Prem Jose Vazhacharickal[1]*, John Joseph[2] and Revathy Krishna[2]
* premjosev@gmail.com
[1]Department of Biotechnology, Mar Augusthinose College, Ramapuram, Kerala, India-686576

[2]Department of Bioscience, Indira Gandhi College of Arts and Science, Nellikuzhi, Kerala, India-686691

Abstract

The study was designed to investigate the antimicrobial and anti-inflammatory efficiency of aqueous extract of dried papaya and castor seeds, which are known to possess various therapeutic properties and economical applications. Microtiter Plate Assay method was used to find out antimicrobial analysis. The aqueous extract has a good antibacterial activity against *Staphylococcus aureus* and the inhibitory percentage for papaya and castor are 79.9% and 85% respectively with the maximum concentration used in this. The anti-inflammatory action is done by HRBC Membrane Stabilization Assay and papaya and castor seed extract showed 56% and 46% inhibition with the maximum concentration used in this. Thus the seeds can be suggested us the preventive agents in diseases and conditions like cancer, edema, tumour, diabetics, anti-viral, cardiovascular diseases, neuro- degenerative diseases to certain extent.

Keywords: *Staphylococcus aureus*, *Carica papaya* L., *Ricinus communis*, Anti-microbial.

1. Introduction

In recent years, the growing demand for herbal products has led to a quantum jump in volume of plant materials traded across the countries. Therefore, the use and history of herbs dates back to the time of early man, who had the crudest tools as his implements and use stones to start his fire. They used herbs in their raw and cooked forms to keep fit. Since that time, the use of herbs has been known and accepted by all nations and has been known also as the first art of treatment available to man. The importance of herbs in the management of human ailments cannot be over emphasized. It is clear that the plant kingdom harbours an inexhaustible source of active ingredients invaluable in the management of many intractable diseases. Furthermore, the active components of herbal remedies have the advantage of being combined with other substances that appear to be inactive. However, these complementary components give the plant as a whole a safety and efficiency much superior to that of its isolated and pure active components.

There is no plant that does not have medicinal value. The active components are normally extracted from all plant structures, but the concentrations of these components vary from structure to structure. However, parts known to contain the highest concentration of the principles are preferred to therapeutic purposes and it can either be the leaves, stems, barks, roots, bulks, corms, rhizomes, woods, flowers, fruits or the seeds. Some of the active principles singly or in combination inhibit greatly the life processes of microbes, especially the disease causing ones. They do this by binding their protein molecules, acting as chelating agents (selective binding polyvalent metal ions so that the latter loses its biological activities), altering their biochemical systems, preventing utilization of available interests to the microorganisms, other causes inflammation analysis of microbial cells. The bitter taste, pungent and repulsive smell in some plants; have been found to have repressive ability over the metabolic activities of a wide range of microorganisms defined medicinal plants as a plant in which one or more of the organs contains substances that can be used for therapeutic purposes or which it precursors for the manufacturing of drugs are useful for disease therapy. The use of medicinal plants predates the introduction of antibiotics and other modern drugs into the African continent. Since medicinal plants do not merely save people from feeling pain but also permit them to emerge unscathed, then they deserve investigation. The active components in these medicinal attribute are expected to be in important to the growth of at least some microorganisms especially the disease causing ones e.g. *Escherichia coli*, *Staphylococcus aureus*, *Proteus mirabilis*, *Klebsiella pneumoniae*, *Pseudomonas aeruginosa* etc. therefore, many studies and researches had been done on the antimicrobial properties of many plants but for this study, the seed of *Carica papaya* and *Ricinus communis* will be discussed (Anibijuwon et al., 2009).

1.1 *Carica papaya* (Papaya)

Pawpaw (*Carica papaya* L.) is the most economically important fruit in the Caricaceae family. It is an erect fast growing and usually unbranched tree or shrub. Although it is native to Central America, it has been transported to many parts of the tropics. The ripe fruit of the pawpaw plant is commonly consumed as food in different parts of the world. However, the unripe fruit is used as mild laxative, for diuresis, as galactogogue and as an abortifacient agent. Many parts of the plant are employed in the treatment of several ailments; for example the seed is used for expelling worms, and the seed and the roots are also used as abortifacient agent. The leaves (especially fallen ones) are used variously for the treatment of fever, pyrexia, diabetes, gonorrhoea, syphilis, inflammation and as dressing for foul wounds. Some of the scientifically validated uses of *C. papaya* include the abortifacient activity of the seeds, the effects of the seeds on germinal epithelium of the seminiferous tubules, the fruit juice for lowering blood pressure, the wound healing effects of the leaves, and several other studies. Papaya fruits, seeds, latex and extracts have been used traditionally to treat various ailments in humans across the world. Papaya seed is found to be a rich source of biologically active isothiocyanate. Unripe pulp of *C. papaya* is rich in carbohydrate and starch and also contains cardenolides and saponins that have medicinal value such as cardenolides used in the treatment of congestive heart failure. Papaya latex showed marked in vivo efficiency against the rodent gastrointestinal nematode, *Heligmosomoides polygyrus*. The seeds are also used as emmenagogue, thirst quenchers, carminatives or for bites and stings of poisonous insects. In Cambodia, Laos and Vietnam, latex is used to treat eczema and psoriasis. Carpaine, an alkaloid with an intensely bitter taste and a strong depressant action on the heart, has been obtained mainly from the leaves, fruit and seeds. In Kelantan (a state of Malaysia), the latex of the unripe fruit is used as a poison for criminal purposes (Anuar et al., 2008).

1.2 Taxonomy of *Carica papaya* Linn (Papaya)

Kingdom: Plantae-- planta, plantes, plants, vegetal

Subkingdom: Tracheobiota

Superdivision: Spermatophyta

Division: Magnoliophyta

Class: Magnoliopsida

Subclass: Dilleniidae

Order: Violales

Family: Caricaceae

Genus: Carica L.

Species: *Carica papaya* L.

1.3 Nutritional value of *Carica papaya* Linn.

Papaya is common's man fruit, which is reasonably priced and has a high nutritive value. It is low in calories and rich in natural vitamins, and minerals. The comparative low calories content (32 Kcal / 100 g of ripe fruit) make this a favourite fruit of obese people who are into weight reducing regime. Papaya has low carotene compared to other fruit such as apples, guava, sitaphal and plantains, which helps to prevent damage by free radicals. Unripe green papaya is used as vegetable, it does not contain carotene but also all other nutrients are present. The fruit is a rich source for different types of enzymes. Papain, vegetable pepsin present in good amount in unripe fruit is an excellent aid to digestion, which helps to digest the protein in food at acid, alkaline and neutral medium. The celiac disease patients, who cannot digest the wheat protein gliandin, can tolerate it, if it is treated with crude papain, papaya has the property of tenderizing meat. This knowledge is being put to use by cooking meat with raw papaya to make it tender and digestible . The fermented papaya fruit is a promising nutraceutical as an antioxidant. It improves the antioxidant defence in elderly patients even without any overt antioxidant deficiency state at the dose of 9 g/day orally. The papaya lipase, a hydrolase enzyme tightly bonded to the water insoluble fraction of crude papain, is considered as a "naturally immobilized" biocatalyst .Papaya markedly increases iron (Fe) absorption from rice meal, which was measured in parous Indian women, using the erythrocyte utilization of radioactive Fe method. The black seeds edible and have a sharp, spicy taste. They are sometimes ground up and used as a substitute for black pepper. In some parts of Asia the young leaves of papaya are steamed and eaten like spinach (Yogiraj et al., 2015).

1.4 Health benefits of papaya

Papaya is a powerhouse of nutrients and is available throughout the year. It is a rich source of three powerful antioxidant vitamin C, vitamin A and vitamin E. The minerals, magnesium and potassium, vitamin B, pantothenic acid and folate and fibre. In addition to all this, it contains a digestive enzyme-papain that effectively treats causes of trauma, allergies and sports injuries. All the nutrients of papaya as a whole improve cardiovascular system, protect against heart diseases, heart attacks, strokes and prevent colon cancer. The fruit is an excellent source of betacarotene that prevents damage caused by free radicals that may cause some forms of cancer. It is reported that it helped in the prevention of diabetic heart disease. Papaya lowers high cholesterol levels as it is a good source of fibre (Vij et al., 2015).

1.5 *Ricinus communis* (Castor)

Castor plant, *Ricinus communis*, is a species of flowering plant in the spurge family, Euphorbiaceae. Its seed is the castor bean which, despite its name, is not a true bean. Castor plant is indigenous to the south eastern Mediterranean Basin, Eastern Africa, and India, but is widespread throughout tropical regions. Although monotypic, the castor oil plant can vary greatly in its growth, habitat and appearance. It is a fast-growing, suckering perennial shrub which can reach the size of a small tree (around 12 meters / 39 feet). If sown early, under glass, and kept at a temperature of around 20 °C (68 °F) until planted out, the castor oil plant can reach a height of 2–3 meters (6.6–9.8 ft) in a year. The flowers are borne in terminal panicle-like inflorescences of green or, in some varieties, shades of red. The oil from the castor seed is colourless or faintly yellow, almost odourless, viscid liquid, having a taste at first bland but subsequently avid and nauseating. The oil extracted from the seed have been used in small doses in clinical setting for numerous medical conditions such as liver and gallbladder disturbances, abscesses, headaches, appendicitis, epilepsy, haemorrhoids, constipation, diarrhoea, intestinal obstructions, skin diseases, hyperactivity in children and to avert threatened abortion in pregnant women.

Traditionally, the Ebira people in Kogi State of Nigeria use it for skin diseases, purgative, heal irritated or inflamed nipples and to aid delivery in delayed expectant mothers. This study therefore was designed to evaluate the antimicrobial and anti-inflammatory action of castor seed extract.

In China, to recover from rhinitis they instil castor bean latex in the ear of the patient; on the other hand, in Madagascar they use the leaves locally in the treatment of angina. Durante describes the custom practised in Italy to splash leaves of the castor bean with vinegar to cure chest inflammation. In Haiti they use castor oil with an infusion of orange leaves against bronchitis. In India and Pakistan, unspecified parts of the plant are used to treat bronchitis. In the Ivory Coast and Upper Volta, to recover from pneumonia and other feverish afflictions, they rub themselves with the leaves. Pierre-Noel states that in Haiti asthma is treated by a spoonful of castor oil with parsley, the effect being immediate; the same weakness is treated in Madagascar with the leaves and in India and Pakistan with unspecified parts of the plant. In India the root is used against pleurodynia. The above-mentioned uses can be partially justified by observations made in the laboratory that extracts of the leaves possess specific activity against *Mycobacterium tuberculosis* and *Aspergillus niger*. The action of terpenic esters present in different amounts in plants of the Euphorbiaceae should be noted.

1.6 Taxonomy of *Ricinus communis* (Castor)

Kingdom: Plantae-- planta, plantes, plants, vegetal

Subkingdom: Viridiplantae

Superdivision: Embryophyta

Division: Tracheophyta

Class: Magnoliopsida

Order: Malpighiales

Family: Euphorbiaceae

Genus: Ricinus L.

Species: *Ricinus communis*

1.7 Cardiovascular apparatus

In 10th century in Iran, the oil was used for apoplexy, and in Haiti, together with the juice of the paiscongo (*Cajanus indica*), the oil is suggested for cerebral congestion. In Ceylon congestions are treated by rubbing with castor oil (instantly warming the blood), whilst in Haiti lymphangitis is treated by lubricating the inflamed part with castor oil. From the pharmacological point of view, the presence of ricinine, an alkaloid derived from pyridine, and the depressant effect on blood pressure (in the dog) caused by extracts of the trunk should be considered.

1.8 Digestive apparatus

The different parts of the castor bean have many applications for infections of the digestive apparatus. Local application of leaves is suggested for dental caries in Madagascar whilst in South East Africa the Zulu utilize the root in cases of odontalgia. In China, according to Wahnofer, the castor bean is used against swelling of the tongue.

1.9 Articulation, bones and muscles

In Haiti they use the leaves to heal contusions and related inflammations. In Arabia the leaves, dampened with the white of an egg and an onion, and in Columbia leaves with the oil, are always applied locally. Rubbing with oil is practised in Algeria for cases of bone deformities, whilst in the Transvaal, acute osteomyelitis is treated with the oil. In Italy articular pains are treated with the cooked seeds minced in soup of old cockerel. In Indonesia the leaves are applied locally. For Libya., "Mix one handful of castor bean, one of occa cow's butter, one of honey and one of vinegar; smear the mixture on a piece of cloth and put it on the afflicted part. "Also, utilization of the castor bean as an anti-rheumatic is quite well known. In Madagascar they apply the leaves locally, in Arabia a no specified part of the plant is used, in Somaliland the oil, and in Ceylon the afflicted part is massaged with the oil cooked with several drugs- if the condition is very serious one tablespoon should be taken for immediate relief. According to Dastur, in India and Pakistan they use a decoction of the roots with potassium carbonate. Watt and Breyer-Brandwijk mention that in India they often use the root against rheumatism, lumbago and sciatica. In the Philippines they use the seeds. In Malaysia the oily leaves or the oil of the leaves are applied to the afflicted part, making sure that if the skin is corroded by it, the skin must also be treated. In Haiti the leaves dipped with castor oil or sheep or pork fat are used to massage the afflicted limbs. The local application of the leaves as an anti-rheumatic draws our attention.

1.10 Urinary tract infections

In Italy the roots of the castor bean are known also for their diuretic action. In India and Pakistan the castor bean is used against inflammation of the genital organs and in particular the purified seed is used against vaginal and uterine diseases. In India the oil is considered to have a spermatopoietic action. In Brazil the root is used against pains due to renal calculus, whilst in Algeria they use a decoction of leaves. In Ceylon, in the case of hydrocele, the oil is massaged on the afflicted part. We should remember that an important polyacetylenic derivative has been isolated from the root extract; moreover, the anti-inflammatory action could be due to the toxic action of ricine, which causes vasodilatation followed by an increase of the platelets.

1.11 Dermatology

Against tinea and seborrhea of the scalp in Ethiopia they smear the oil locally again, the oil in an alcoholic solution is employed in Italy as it is recognised to have an anti-seborrheic action and favours the growth of hair. In Angola the leaves are used externally to treat scabies and skin diseases. In Guinea Bissau the oil is obtained from the decorticated seeds by boiling in water, following which the oil that is floating is collected by means of decantation, and is used against dermatosis and itch (scabies). Among the Basutos in South Africa, the roasted seeds are pulverized to treat impetigo, eczema and pustules. In Tanganyika the young leaves are used to treat furuncles. In Africa (Tonga-Mozambique) the juice of the cortex of the castor bean is put on eruptions of the skin, whilst a drink of the minced cortex is used against pustules. China the juice of the leaves is put on chronic wounds of the legs. In India and Pakistan they use the mashed seeds against scrofulous ulcers; in the Philippines, again against ulcers, the leaves are cooked in milk to make a mash which is applied locally. In Columbia the oil is the ideal application against ulcerated feet. In the field of cosmetology we are reminded that in Italy the oil is used in an alcoholic solution 1773 and in Tanganyika they use it to grease the body with soap and oil. Here we assume that only some of the substances contained in the castor bean can have a biodynamic activity in the field of dermatology.

1.12 Venereal diseases

The crushed seeds of the castor bean are used in Eritrea to treat blennorrhagia. In the Dominican Republic the seeds are used as a decoction against gonorrhoea. In India and Pakistan, whilst used against the same venereal disease, no precise information is available as to which part of the plant is used. In Algeria, the pulverized seeds are swallowed with honey to treat syphilis. The effect goes on for one year for every seed swallowed after preparing it in the warm blood of rabbit. Recently, ricin has been localized electrophoretically in the beta-globulin band. It most probably provides a barrier, though weak, with an immunological action that seems to be effective against the formation of tumours, as already mentioned.

1.13 Ophthalmology

In Nigeria, castor oil is used to-prepare, as a soothing base, ophthalmic compounds. In India and Pakistan the oil is used locally against conjunctivitis. For inflammation of the eye in Indonesia they apply the leaves locally. In Columbia one drop of oil in the eye reduces reddening and inflammation; one drop put on the eyelids treats sties. Finally, in Italy the green leaves, with maize pudding, relieves inflammation of the eyes. We have already referred above to the anti-inflammatory action of the pharmacological derivatives of the castor bean (Scarpa et al., 1980).

1.14 *Staphylococcus aureus*

Staphyloccoccus aureus ("grape cluster berry" , Latin aureus , "golden") is a facultative anaerobic gram-positive coccal bacterium also known as "golden saph" and Oro staphira. In medical literature the bacteria is often referred to as *S. aureus* or *Staph aureus. Staphlococcus aureus* should not be confused with the similarly named and medically relevant genus Streptococcus.

S. aureus appears as grape-like clusters when viewed through a microscope, and has large, round, golden yellow colonies, often with haemolysis, when grown on blood agar plates. S aureus reproduces asexually by binary fission. Two daughter cells do not fully separate and remain attached to one another. This is why the cells are observed in clusters.

S aureus is catalase positive. Catalase converts hydrogen peroxide to water and oxygen. Catalase activity tests are sometimes used to distinguish staphylococci from enterococci and streptococci. Previously S aureus was differentiated from other staphylococci by coagulase test. However it is now known that not all S aureus are coagulase positive and that are incorrect species identification can impact effective treatment and control measures.

S. aureus is responsible for many infections but it may also occur as a commensal. The presence of S. aureus does not always indicate infection. S aureus can survive for hours to weeks or even months, on dry environmental surfaces, depending on strain. S aureus can infect tissues when the skin or mucosal barriers have been breached. This can lead to many different types of infections including furuncles and carbuncles (a collection of furuncles). S. aureus infections can spread through contact with pus from an infected wound, skin to skin contact with an infected person by producing hyaluronidase that destroys tissues, and contact with objects such as towels, sheets, clothing, or athletic equipment used by an infected person. Deeply penetrating S. aureus infections can be severe. Strains of *S. aureus* can host phages such as Φ- PVL (produces Panton – Valentine leukocidin) that increases virulence.

1.15 Aim

The aim of this study is to evaluate the anti-microbial and anti-inflammatory role of astor and Papaya seeds against *Staphylococcus aureus*.

1.16 Objectives

The objectives of the current research work are to characterize and evaluate the phytochemical and antimicrobial activity of Castor and Papaya against *Staphylococcus aureus*.

2. Review of literature

In recent years, the growing demand for herbal products has led to a quantum jump in volume of plant materials traded across the countries. Papaya (*Carica papaya* L.) is a plant that grows wild in many parts of the tropics. Papaya is important for its fruit and it is cultivated mainly for this purpose. Papaya is also grown for papain production. *Carica papaya* belongs to the family Caricaceae. It has the following common names; pawpaw tree, papaya, papayer, tinti, pepol, chich put, fan kua, wan shoukuo, kavunagaci, kepaya etc. The parts that are usually used include the leaves, fruit, seed, latex, and root. The plant is described as a fast growing, erect, usually unbranched tree or shrub, 7-8 m tall with copious latex, trunk of about 20 cm in diameter. The plant is also described in a documented property forms and it act as analgesic, amoebicide, antibacterial, cardiotonic, cholagogue, digestive, emenagogue, febrifuge, hypotensive, laxative, pectoral, stomachic and vermifuge. *Carica papaya* contains many biochemically active compounds. Two important compounds are chymopapain and papain, which are supposed to aid in digestion.

Papain is used in the treatment of arthritis. The leaves of *Carica papaya* is used as soap substitute which are supposed to remove stains. The papain, the proteolytic enzyme has a wealth of industrial uses. It has milk clotting (rennet) and protein digesting properties. Active over a wide pH range, papain is used in medicine, combating dyspepsia and other digestive orders. In liquid preparations, it has been used for reducing enlarged tonsils. Nearly 80% of American beer is treated with papain, which digests the precipitable protein fragmented and then the beer remains clear on cooling. Papain is also used for degumming natural silk. But most of the papain imported in the U.S is used for meat-tenderizers and chewing gums. Also used to extract the oil from tuna liver cosmetically, it is used in some dentifrices, shampoos and face-lifting preparations. Use to cleat silks and wools before dying and to remove hair from hides during tanning (James, 1983). it is also used in the manufacture of rubber from heaven. Recently, FDA has cleared chymopapain for intradiscal injection in patients with documented herniated lumbar inter-vertebral discs whose signs and symptoms have not responded to conservative therapy over an adequate period of time. The medicinal folk uses the leaves poultice onto nervous pains and elephantoid growths. The leaf smoked for asthma relief in various remote areas. Javanese believe that eating papaya prevent rheumatism. Dietary papaya does reduce urine acidity in humans while the flowers have been used for jaundice. The young leaves and to lesser degree other parts contain carpain an active bitter alkaloid which has a depressing action on heart. The plant is strong amoebicide. The efficacy of treatment with C. papaya is dependent on the quantity of the different compounds in the preparations. In Indonesia, papaya leaves are used as feed for animals after parturition-2 leaves boiled in water fed every 2 days for 1week. It also has been reported that papaya leaf extracts is used as a profilaxis against malaria, though no studies on this use could be found in the literature . In Nigeria, it is used for smooth upper respiratory tract ailment and tumour (uterus). In Ivory Coast, it is used for treating madness. In Trinidad, it is used for treating scorpion bites and hypertension. In cote d'Ivoire and Sama, it is used for toothache and tuberculosis in Mexico. In Honduras and Turkey, it is used for liver ailments, constipation and laxative. In Philippines, India, Malagasy and Malaya, it is used for treating arthritis and rheumatism. In Java, Panama, Sri Lanka and Turkey, it is used for treating abortifacient. In Honduras, Japan, Panama and West Africa, it is used for the treatment of diarrhoea and dysentery.

2.1 Benefits

The traditional use of papaya to treat many diseases, especially skin conditions and its prohibition for consumption during pregnancy has prompted us to determine whether papaya extracts both from green and ripe fruits improve wound healing and also produce foetal toxicity. Aqueous extracts of green papaya epicarp (GPE) and ripe papaya epicarp (RPE) were applied on induced wounds on mice. GPE treatment induced complete healing in shorter periods (13 days) than that required while using RPE (17 days), sterile water (18 days) and Solcoseryl ointment (21 days). Extracts were administered orally (1 mg/g body weight/day) to pregnant mice from day 10 and onwards after conception. 3 (n = 7) mice and 1 (n = 6) mice given RPE and misoprostol, an abortive drug, respectively experienced embryonic resorption while this effect was observed in none of the mice given GPE (n = 5) and water (n = 5). The average body weight of live pups delivered by mice given GPE (1.12 ± 0.04 g) was significantly lower than those delivered by mice given water (1.38 ± 0.02 g). In SDS–PAGE, proteins were distributed in three bands (Mrrange 8–29 kDa). Band intensity at Mr 28–29 kDa was higher in GPE than in RPE. In contrast, band intensity at low Mr (8 kDa) was found to be higher in RPE than in GPE. Notably, the band corresponding to Mr 23–25 kDa was absent in RPE. These differences in composition may have contributed to the different wound healing and abortive effects of green and ripe papaya.

2.2 Antioxidant activity

The methanolic extract of unripe fruits of *C. papaya* was evaluated in vivo for its effect on activities of some antioxidant enzymes which includes glutathione peroxidase and formaldehyde induced arthritis models. The ulcerogenic activity of the extract was also investigated. The result showed that the extract at the dose of 25-250 mg/kg p.o exhibited significant reduction in the paw edema in the carrageenan test. The extract produced slight mucosal irritation at higher doses.

2.3 Antimicrobial activity

The aqueous extract of C. papaya leaves and roots at different concentrations (25, 50,100,200 mg/L) showed antimicrobial activity against some human pathogenic bacteria using the agar diffusion method.

2.4 Antifungal activity

The latex of *C. papaya* and fluconazole has synergistic action on the inhibition of *Candida albicans* growth. This synergistic effect results in partial cell wall degradation. Latex proteins appear to be responsible for antifungal action and minimum protein concentration for producing a complete inhibition was reported as about 138 mg/mL.

2.5 Antifertility activity

The crude extract of bark of C. papaya [5-10 mL/(kg.d), p.o for 4 weeks] on the seminiferous tubules of rats showed complete loss of fertility attributing to decline in sperm motility and alteration in their morphology. Thus the bark showed the safe and could serve as an effective male contraceptive in animals.

2.6 Wound healing activity

The aqueous extract of *C. papaya* fruit [100 mg/ (kg.d) for 10 d] for wound healing property in streptozotocin-induced diabetic rats using excision and dead space wound models. The aqueous extract shows 77% reduction in the wound area when compared to 59% contraction to wound of the controls. Thus the result suggested that the aqueous extract of *C .papaya* had a potent wound healing property.

2.7 Anti-tumour activity

The aqueous The aqueous extract of C. papaya leaves (0.625-20 mg/ mL) exhibits anti-tumour activity. The extract significantly inhibited the proliferative responses of solid tumour cell lines derived from cervical carcinoma (Hela), breast adenocarcinoma (MCF-7), hepatocellular carcinoma (HepG2), lung adenocarcinoma (PCl4), pancreatic epithelial carcinoma (Panc-1) and mesothelioma (H2452) in a dose dependent manner.

2.8 Anti-malarial activity

The petroleum ether extract of the rind of raw papaya fruit at concentration ranging from 0.05-1 000 µg/mL. The extract exhibited significant anti-malarial activity.

2.9 *Ricinus communis* (Castor)

Ricinus communis Linn. (Euphorbiaceae) is a soft-wooded small tree widespread throughout tropics and warm temperature regions of the world. In the Indian system of medicine, the leaf, root and seed o l of this plant have been used for the treatment of inflammation In the Indian system of medicine, the leaf, root and seed oil of this plant have been used for the treatment of inflammation and liver disorders as they have been found to be hepatoprotective, hypoglycemic, laxative, diuretic (Abraham et al., 1986) and antibacterial.

2.10 Benefits of Castor seeds

The castor oil obtained from the seed of the plant is still widely used traditionally and herbally as a medicine. The seed of the plant is used as fertilizer after the oil was extracted cooked to destroy the toxin and incorporated into animal feeds. The principal use of castor oil is as a purgative and laxative. It is also used as a lubricant, lamp fuel, a component of cosmetics, and in the manufacture of soaps, printer's ink, plastics, fibres, hydraulic fluid, brake fluid, varnishes, paints, embalming fluid, textile dyes, leather finishes, adhesives, waxes, and fungicides. In India, the leaves are used as food for eri silk worms and the stalks are used for fuel purpose. This species has been planted for its dune stabilization properties.

2.11 Anti-asthmatic activity

The ethanolic root extract of *R. communis* is effective in treatment of asthma because of its antiallergic and mast cell stabilizing potential effect. Saponins has mast cell stabilizing effect and the flavonoids possess smooth muscle relaxant and bronchodilator activity; the apigenin and luteolin like flavonoids were generally inhibit basophil histamine release and neutrophils beta glucuronidase release, and finally shows in-vivo antiallergic activity. The *R. communis* ethanolic extract decreases milk induced leucocytosis and eosinophilia and possess anti-asthmatic activity due to presence of flavonoids or saponins.

2.12 Anti-fertility activity

The methanol extracts of *R. communis* seed possess positive preliminarily phytochemical tests for both steroids and alkaloids. The pituitary gland releases gonadotrophins due to Sex hormones by both positive and negative feedback mechanism and also the pituitary gland block the release of luteinizing hormone (LH) and the follicle-stimulating hormone (FSH) because of the effect of combined oestrogen and progesterone in the luteal phase of the menstrual cycle. Finally it helps the inhibition of maturation of the follicle in the ovary and prevents ovulation. The sex hormone being steroidal compound's (phytosterols) and the presence of steroids in methanol extract of *Ricinus communis* seed produces anti-fertility effects.

2.13 Anti-histaminic activity

The ethanol extract of *R. communis* root resulted anti histaminic activity at the dose 100, 125, and 150 mg/kg intraperitoneally by using clonidine induced catalepsy in mice 21.

2.14 Invitro immune modulatory activity

The plant and animal origin immune modulatory agents generally increase the immune responsiveness of the human body against pathogens by activating the non-specific immune system. The phagocytosis is the engulfment of microorganism by leucocytes. In last the phagocytosis is the intracellular killing of microorganisms by the neutrophils. The presence of tannins in the leaves of *R. communis* significantly increased the phagocytic function of human neutrophils and resulted produces a possible immune modulatory effect.

2.15 Hepatoprotective activity

Ricinus communis leaves ethanolic extract 250/500mg/kg body weight possesses hepatoprotective activity due to their inhibitory activities of an increase in the activities of serum transaminases and the level of liver lipid per oxidation, protein, glycogen and the activities of acid and alkaline phosphatase in liver induced by carbon tetrachloride (CCL4). The *R. communis* ethanolic extract 250/500mg/kg body weight also treated the depletion of glutathione level and adenosine triphosphatase activity which was observed in the CCl4-induced rat liver. The presence of flavonoids in ethanol extract of *R. communis* produces beneficial effect the flavonoids have the membrane stabilizing and antiperoxidative effects. Hence the *R. communis* increase the regenerative and reparative capacity of the liver due to the presence of flavonoids and tannins. The anticholestatic and hepatoprotective activity was seen against paracetamol-induced hepatic damage due to the presence of N-demethylricinine isolated from the leaves of *Ricinus communis* Linn. The whole leaves of *Ricinus communis* showed the protective effect against liver necrosis as well as fatty changes induced by CCL4 while the glycoside and cold aqueous extract provide protection only against liver necrosis and fatty changes respectively.

2.16 Anti-inflammatory activity

Anti-inflammatory activities of the leaves and root extract were studied in Whistar albino rats in acute and chronic inflammatory models. The study indicated that the paw edema formation due to sub plantar administration of carragennan, characterizing the cellular events of acute inflammation. The 250 and 500 mg/kg dose of *R. communis* methanolic leaves extract possess protective effect in prevention of cellular events during edema formation and in all the stages of acute inflammation. The anti-inflammatory activity of *R. communis* methanolic extract was due to the presence of flavonoids because the flavonoids have the protective effect against carragennan-induced paw edema in rats.

2.17 Anti-oxidant activity

It is concluded that *R. communis* antioxidant activity by using lipid method and free radical scavenging effect on 2,2picrylhydrazyl radical (DPPH) and hydroxyl hydrogen peroxide. The high antioxidant activity of the seed of *R. communis* at low concentration shows that it could be very useful for the treatment of disease resulting from oxidative stress. The responsible chemical constituent of antioxidant activity are Methyl ricinoleate, Ricinoleic acid, 12 octadecadienoic acid and methyl ester stem and leave extracts also produce antioxidant activity due to the presence of flavonoids in their extracts

2.18 Anti-microbial activity

The antimicrobial activities of *Ricinus communis* were good against dermatophytic and pathogenic bacterial strains *Streptococcus progenies*, *Staphylococcus aureus* as well as *Klebsiella pneumonia*, *Escherichia coli*. The result showed that the petroleum ether and acetone extracts possess good zone of inhibition where as ethanolic extract having anti-bacterial activity only on higher concentration30. The different solvent extracts of roots of *Ricinus communis* (200mg/ml) possess antimicrobial activity by using well diffusion method against pathogenic microorganisms such as *Escherichia coli*, *Staphylococcus aureus*, *Pseudomonas aeruginosa*, *Salmonella typhimurium*, *Proteus vulgaris*, *Bacillus subtilis*, *Candida albicans* and *Aspergillus niger*. The hexane and methanol extracts showed maximum antimicrobial activity where the aqueous extracts has no significant antimicrobial properties.

2.19 Anti-diabetic activity

The ethanolic extract of roots of *Ricinus communis* (RCRE) was investigated along with its bioassay-guided purification. By administration of the effective dose (500mg/kg b. w) of RCRE to the diabetic rats for 20 days possess favourable effects not only on fasting blood glucose, but also on total lipid profile and liver and kidney functions. Amongst all fractions the R-18 fraction suggests the significant antihyperglycemic activity. RCRE showed no significant difference in alkaline phosphatase, serum bilirubin, creatinine, serum glutamate oxaloacetate transaminases, serum glutamate pyruvate transaminases and total protein which was observed even after the administration of the extract at a dose of 10 g/kg b.wt. Thus *R. communis* is a potent phytomedicine for diabetes32.

2.20 Wound healing activity

The *Ricinus communis* possess wound healing activity due to the active constituent of castor oil which produce antioxidant activity and inhibit lipid per oxidation. Those agents whose inhibits lipid per oxidation is believed to increase the viability of collagen fibrils by increasing the strength of collagen fibres, increasing the circulation, preventing the cell damage and by promoting the DNA synthesis. The study of wound healing activity of castor oil was in terms of scar area, % closure of scar area and epithelization in excision wound model. Due to the astringent and antimicrobial property the tannins, flavonoids, triterpenoids and sesquiterpenes promotes the wound healing process, which are responsible for wound contraction and increased rate of epithelialisation. The study resulted that the Castor oil showed wound healing activity by reducing the scar area and also the epithelization time in excision wound model. The comparison study of two different concentrations (5%w/w and 10%w/w) of castor oil was resulted that the 10 % w/w Castor oil ointment possesses better wound-healing property.

2.21 Lipolytic activity

The ricin produces the lipolytic activity by using the various substrates: (i) one analogue of triacylglycerol, BAL-TC4; (ii) various chromogenic substrates such as p-NP esters of aliphatic short to medium chain acids, and (iii) mono molecular films of a pure natural diacylglycerol, DC10 in emulsion and in a Membrane-like model. The study concluded that ricin from *R. communis* act as a lipase and has the capability of hydrolyzing different lipid classes. Ricin also hydrolyses phospholipids which are the major components of cellular membranes. The lipolytic activities are maximal at pH 7.0 in the presence of 0.2 M galactose. The action of ricin on membrane phospholipids could occur through a phospholipase A1 activity which is very often a minor activity of lipases.

2.22 Molluscidal, insecticidal and larvicidal activity

The leaf extract of *R. communis* possess molluscicidal activity against Lymnaea acuminata and the seed extracts showed better insecticidal and insectistatic activity than the leaf extracts against *S. frugiperda* due to the active ingredients like castor oil and ricinine. The aqueous leaves extracts of *R. communis* possess suitable larvicidal activity against *Anopheles arabiensis*, *Calloso bruchuschinensis* and *Culex quinquefasciatus* mosquitoes.

2.23 Antiulcer activity

The castor oil of *R. communis* seed possess significant antiulcer properties at a dose of 500 mg/kg and 1000 mg/kg, but at the dose 1000 mg/kg was more potent against the ulceration caused by pylorus ligation, aspirin and ethanol in rats. The result showed that the antiulcer activity of *R. communis* is due to the cytoprotective action of the drug or strengthening of gastric mucosa and thus enhancing the mucosal defence.

3. Hypothesis

The current research work is based on the following hypothesis

1) Castor and papaya seeds possess anti-microbial and anti-inflammatory activity against *Staphylococcus aureus*.

4. Materials and Methods

4.1 Study area

Kerala state covers an area of 38,863 km^2 with a population density of 859 per km^2 and spread across 14 districts. The climate is characterized by tropical wet and dry with average annual rainfall amounts to 2,817 ± 406 mm and mean annual temperature is 26.8°C (averages from 1871-2005; Krishnakumar et al., 2009). Maximum rainfall occurs from June to September mainly due to South West Monsoon and temperatures are highest in May and November.

4.2 Collection and extraction of samples

In this study, Fresh and ripe seeds of papaya and castor was collected and dried to use as material of study. The dried seeds are extracted by soxhlet extraction apparatus.

4.3 Phytochemical analysis

Phytochemical progress has been aided enormously by the development of rapid and accurate methods of screening plants for particular chemicals.

4.3.1 Estimation of flavonoids

A portion of the crude extract was heated with ethyl acetate over a steam bath for 3minutes.The mixture was filtered and 4ml of the filtrate was shaken with 1ml dil. ammonia solution and observed for yellow coloration.

4.3.2 Estimation of terpenoids

The extract was mixed with 2ml of chloroform and 3ml conc. H_2SO_4 is added carefully along the sides of the test tube to form a layer. A reddish brown colouration at the interface indicates positive results.

4.3.3 Estimation of steroids

0.5g crude extract was dissolved in methanol and cooled in ice. This was mixed with 0.5ml chloroform and 1ml con. $H_2SO_4$was then added carefully by means of a pipette.

At the layer of separation of 2 liquids a reddish brown colour was formed indicating the presence of steroids.

4.3.4 Estimation of cardiac glycosides

Keller Killiani Test: 5ml of methanolic extract with 2ml of glacial acetic acid containing 1 drop of ferric chloride solution followed by the addition of 1ml conc. H_2SO_4. A brown ring was formed at the interface indicating the presence of deoxy sugar cardinolides. A violet ring may appear beneath the brown ring.

4.3.5 Estimation of proteins

Biuret Test: The extract was treated with 1ml of 1% NaOH solution and heated. A drop of 0.7% copper sulfate solution is added to the above solution. The formation of purplish violet colour indicated the presence of proteins.

4.3.6 Estimation of amino acids

To the extract 0.25% Ninhydrin reagent is added and boiled for a few minutes. Formation of blue color indicates the presence of amino acids.

4.3.7 Estimation of carbohydrates

The extract was shaken vigorously with water and then filtered. To the aqueous filtrate a few drops of molischers reagent was added followed by vigorous shaking, 1 ml concentrated sulphuric acid was added to form a layer bellow the aqueous solution. A brown ring at the interface indicates the presence of carbohydrates.

4.3.8 Estimation of phenols

2 ml of test solution in alcohol was added with 1 drop of neutral ferric chloride solution. Formation of intense blue color indicates the presence of phenol.

4.3.9 Estimation of alkaloids

Drangendroffs test: A fraction of the extract was treated with Dragendroffs reagent and observed for the formation of reddish orange precipitate.

4.3.10 Detection of saponins

Foam test: A fraction of extract was vigorously shaken with water, observed for persistent foam.

4.4 Microtitre plate assay

- Papaya and castor seeds extract were taken in separate containers.
- Microtitre for the test is also taken and opened in the LAF.

- Mark the wells in one row with test from T_1 to T_4, and mark corresponding controls against each test from C_1 to C_2 below the row.
- Use *S. aureus* as culture.
- Increasing concentration of papaya seed extract from 25µl to 100µlis placed in each wells of test(T_1 to T_4).
- To all wells of test add 100µl culture and 100µl Nutrient broth.
- To all corresponding controls(C_1 to C_4) add increasing volume from 25µl to 100µl seed extract and to all controls add 100µl of nutrient broth.
- A common control is placed (C).
- To this control(C) add 100µl culture and 100µl nutrient broth.
- Keep it for incubation at 37°c for 24hrs.
- Obtain the OD (640nm) value from UV-vis spectrometry.
- Percentage of inhibition from T_1 to T_2 is obtained by calculation, which is obtained by using the equation;

  Percentage of inhibition(%) = $\underline{\text{Control} - \text{Test}^*}$ ×100

  Control

  $$[\text{Test}^* = T_1 - C_1]$$
- Same procedure is followed or castor seed extract.

4.4.1 Anti-inflammatory activity (HRBC membrane stabilisation assay)

- Collect 10ml of blood.
- Allow it to clot by leaving it undisturbed at room temperature.
- Centrifuge it at 3000rpm for 10minutes.
- Collect the supernatant (serum).
- Measure the volume of serum and prepare 10% V/v suspension with normal saline.
- Then arrange tubes for the further steps.
- Papaya seed extract is taken.
- Mark the tubes from T_1 to$T_3$for Test and a common control (C) is placed.
- To each test from T_1 to T_3 add increasing concentration of papaya seed extract from 25µl to150µl.

- Add 50µl culture and 1ml HRBC Suspension to all tests.

- Keep it for incubation at room temperature for an hour.

- Obtain the OD (540nm) in calorimetry

- Percentage of inhibition is calculated for each tests by using the equation;

Percentage of inhibition $=\underline{\text{Control- Test}} \times 100\%$

Control

4.5 Statistical analysis

The survey results were analysed and descriptive statistics were done using SPSS 12.0 (SPSS Inc., an IBM Company, Chicago, USA) and graphs were generated using Sigma Plot 7 (Systat Software Inc., Chicago, USA).

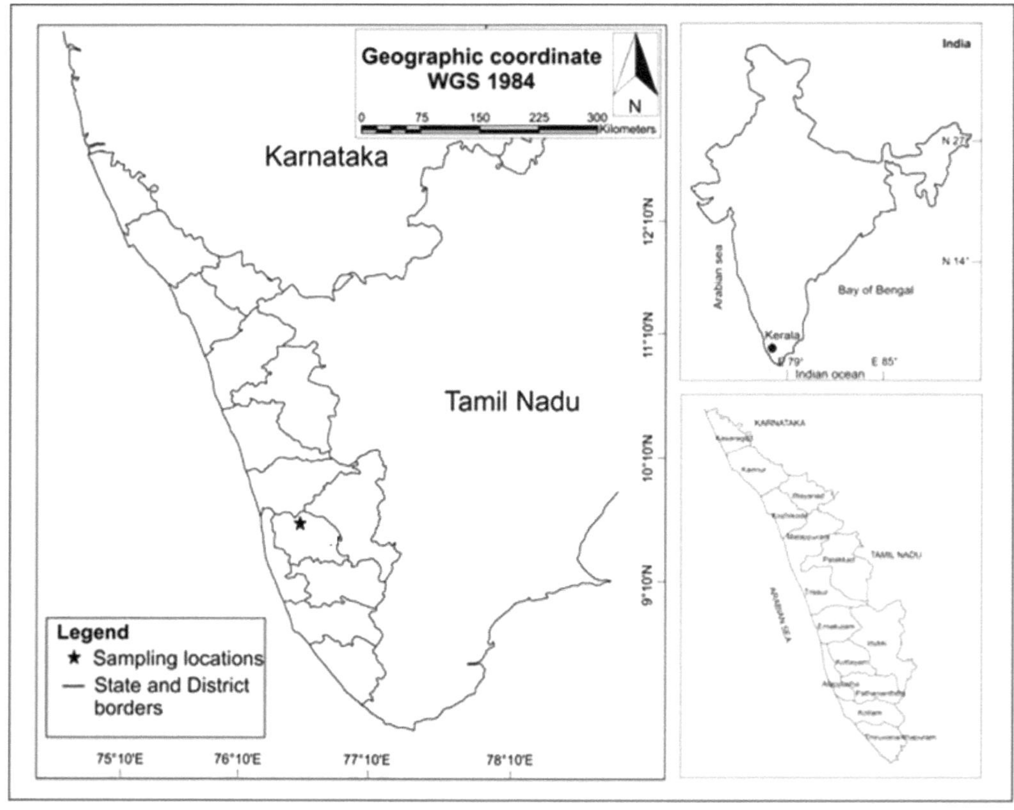

Figure 1. Map of Kerala showing the sample collection point. Authors own work.

Figure 2. Papaya (*Carica papaya*) description a) different parts of the tree, b) fruit cut opened, c) tree bearing ripe and half mature fruits, d) young leaves, e) developing flower buds. Photo courtesy: Wikipedia.

Figure 3. Castor (*Ricinus communis*) description a) different parts of the plant, b) fruit cut opened, c) young leaves, d) tree bearing ripe and half mature fruits. Photo courtesy: Wikipedia.

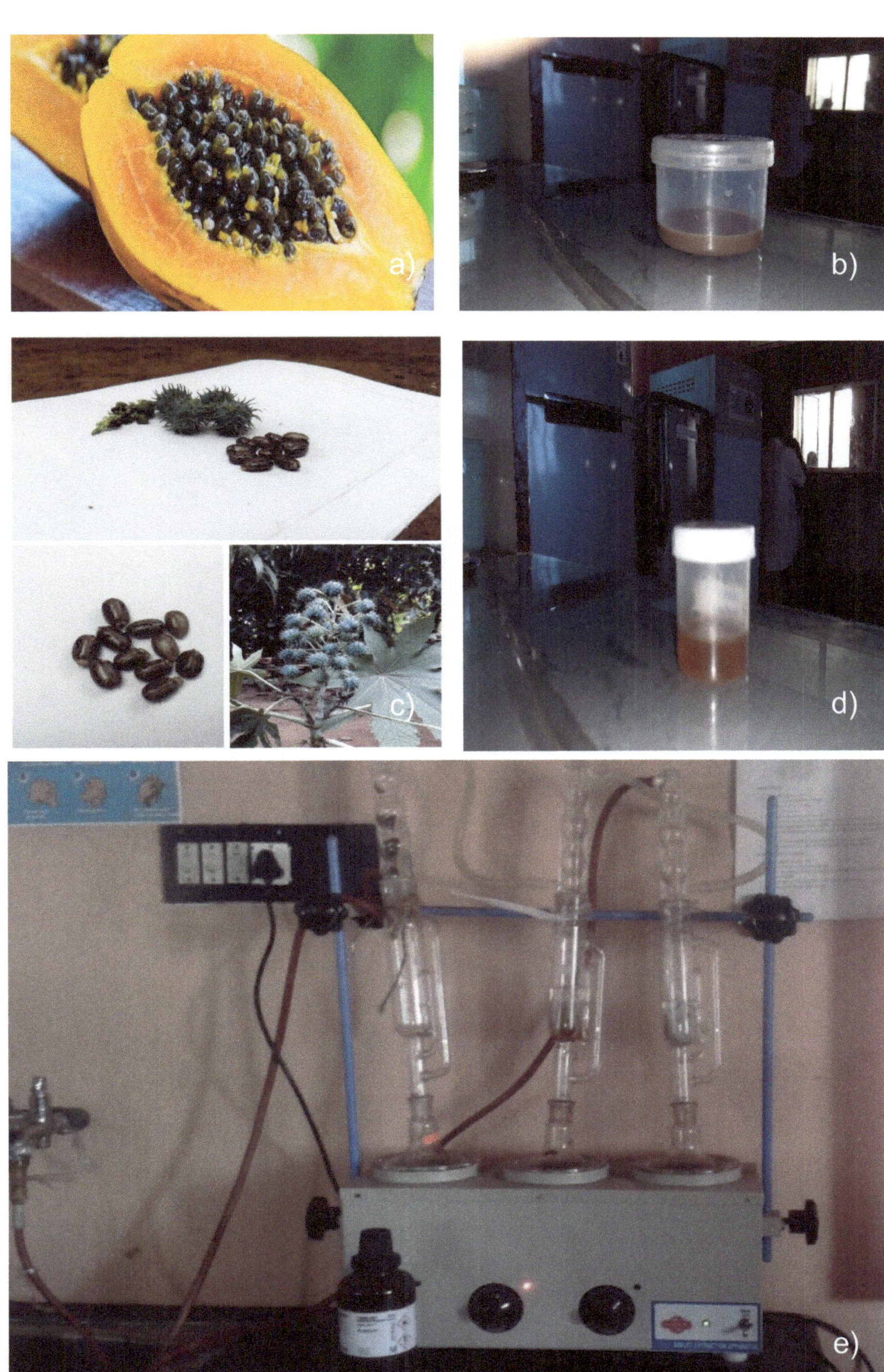

Figure 4. Description of a) Papaya seed, b) Papaya dry seed extract, c) Castor seeds, d) Castor dry seed extract, e) Soxhlet extraction apparatus.

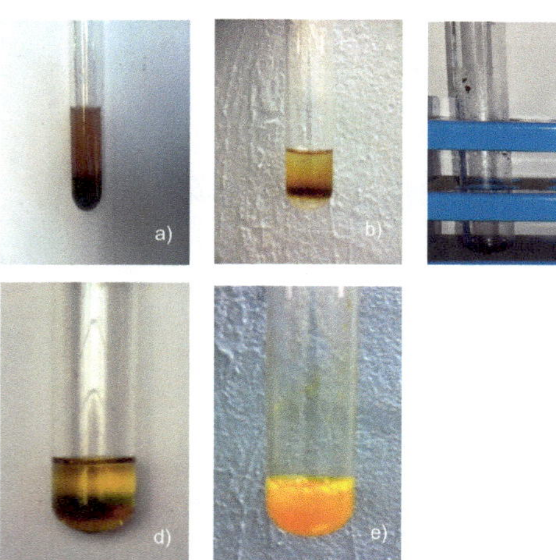

Figure 5. Phytochemical analysis of Papaya dry seed extract a) Terpenoids, b) Steroids, c) Amino acids, d) Carbohydrates, e) Alkaloids.

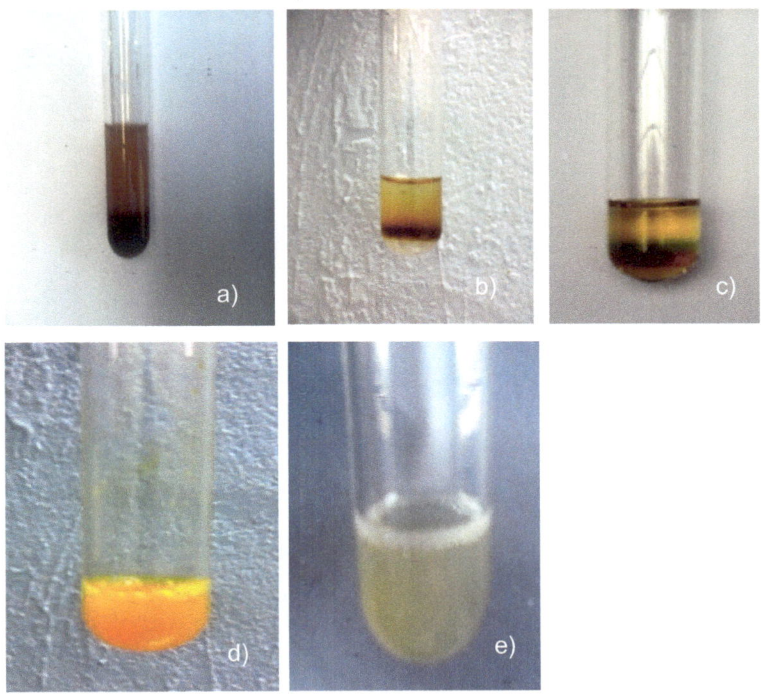

Figure 6. Phytochemical analysis of Castor dry seed extract a) Terpenoids, b) Steroids, c) Carbohydrates, d) Alkaloids, e) Saponins.

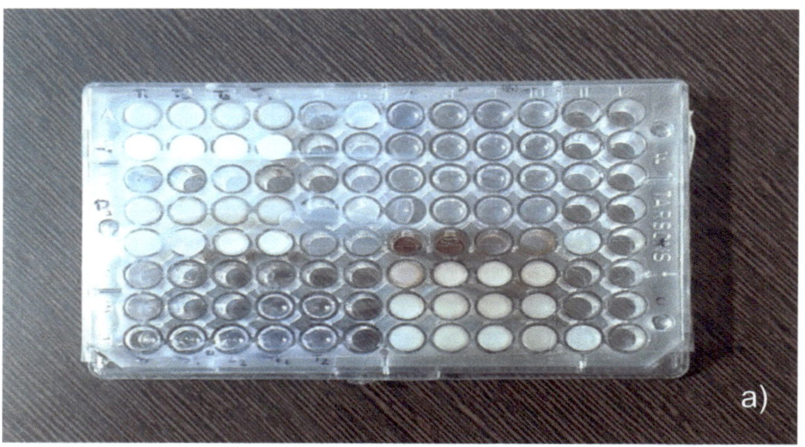

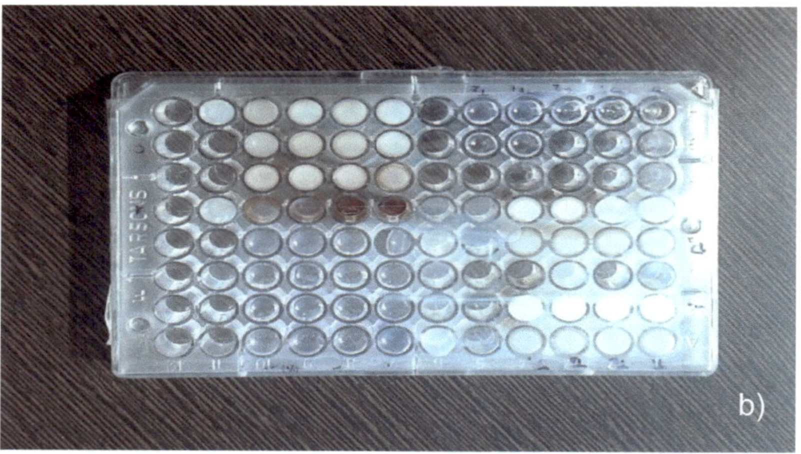

Figure 7. Description of the antimicrobial activity using microtiter plate assay a) Papaya seeds, b) Castor seeds.

Table 1. Description of the phytochemical analysis of Papaya and Castor seeds.

Test	Positive control	Papaya	Castor
Flavonoids	yellow coloration	-	-
Terpenoids	reddish brown colouration	+	+
Steroids	reddish-brown ring	+	+
Cardiac glycosides	brown ring	-	-
Proteins	purplish-violet colour	-	-
Amino acids	blue colour	+	-
Carbohydrates	brown ring	+	+
Phenols	intense blue	-	-
Alkaloids	reddish-orange precipitate	+	+
Saponins	persistent foam	-	+

+: Present; -: Absent

Table 2. Antimicrobial activity of Castor seeds against *S. aureus* using different concentration of extracts.

SL NO	CONCENTRATION OF EXTRACT	OD VALUE OF CONTROL	OD VALUE OF TEST	% OF INHIBITION
1	25 µl	0.988	0.944	77
2	50 µl	0.988	0.787	82
4	75µl	0.988	0.546	84
5	100 µl	0.988	0.281	**85**

Table 3. Antimicrobial activity of Papaya seeds against *S. aureus* using different concentration of extracts.

SL NO	CONCENTRATION OF EXTRACT	OD VALUE OF CONTROL	OD VALUE OF TEST	% OF INHIBITION
1	25 µl	0.988	0.612	11.1
2	50 µl	0.988	0.42	57.4
4	75 µl	0.988	0.314	68.2
5	100 µl	0.988	0.2	79.7

Table 4. Anti-inflammatory activity of Papaya seeds against *S. aureus*.

ST	Conc. of extract	OD	% OF INHIBITION
T$_1$	50 µl	0.60	6%
T$_2$	100 µl	0.45	18%
T$_3$	150 µl	0.23	56%
Control		0.98	

Table 5. Anti-inflammatory activity of Castor seeds against *S. aureus*.

TEST	Conc. of extract	OD	% OF INHIBITION
T$_1$	100 µl	0.72	26%
T$_2$	200 µl	0.64	34%
T$_3$	500 µl	0.52	46%
Control		0.98	

5. Results

Phytochemical tests have been done for both papaya and castor seed extracts. Antimicrobial activity by microtiter plate assay showed increase in the inhibitory action with increase in concentration for both extracts, in which castor seed extract showed more inhibition than papaya seed extract in 100µl.

Anti-Inflammatory by HRBC Membrane Stabilization Assay showed with the increase in the concentration of seed extract it show relevant anti-inflammatory action against the culture (*S. aureus*). Papaya seed extract showed more inhibition than castor seed extract.

6. Discussion

Ricinus communis is well known for its biological activities, most important of which are hepatoprotective, laxative, antidiabetic, antifertility activities. The seeds yield castor oil, which has been used to treat liver infection and to cure inflammation in Indian system of medicine. Papaya is common's man fruit, which is reasonably priced and has a high nutritive value. It is low in calories and rich in natural vitamins, and minerals.

The broader spectrum antimicrobial activities observed could be due to the synergic effect of the various components in the *Ricinus comunis* extract. The antimicrobial mechanism can be attributed to the presence of major phytochemicals that were detected in the studies. The inhibitory effect on the population proliferation of microorganisms were observed at increasing concentrations of flavonoids and tannins in the extracts (Alugah and Ibraheem, 2000). It thus implies that castor plant possess essential phytochemicals, which could be exploited for medicinal or pharmaceutical applications. Extracts of castor plant seeds used in this work show promising antimicrobial properties.

In this study the extract exhibit significant anti-inflammatory activity. The anti-inflammatory activity of *Ricinus comunis* was due to the presence of flavonoids because the flavonoids have the protective effect against inflammation (Ilavarasan et al., 2006; Valderiamas et al., 2008; Anil Kumar Saini et al., 2010). The study of Inoyor and Ibraheem (2014) revealed the presence of phenolics and saponins in *Ricinus communis*. Phenolics and saponins, phytochemicals have been shown to have variety of biological activity in humans. Saponins, saponin glycosides and phenols were found in its extract.

The qualitative preliminary phytochemicals analysis was performed to detect the nature and presence of phytoconstituents in the different parts of the crude solvent and oil extract of *Ricinus communis*. Rahmati et al (2015), studied the methanolic extract of *Ricinus communis* seeds for its in vitro antimicrobial activities through the agar diffusion method. The seed extract of the castor oil plant inhibited the growth of *Staphylococcus aureus*, *Escherichia coli*, *Pseudomonas aeruginosa*, *Salmonella typhi*, *Bacillus subtilis* and *Candida albicans*. In the present study, it also shows the antimicrobial activity against the tested organisms such as *Staphylococcus aureus*,

Escherichia coli, Pseudomonas sp., *Salmonella typhi, Bacillus cereus* and *Candida albicans.* The percentage of inhibition also increase with the concentration.

The black seeds edible and have a sharp, spicy taste. They are sometimes ground up and used as a substitute for black pepper (Vijay Yogiraj ,et al.,2015). It is reported that it helped in the prevention of diabetic heart disease. Papaya lowers high cholesterol levels as it is a good source of fibre (Vij et al., 2015).

In the present study, Papaya showed the presence of phytochemicals like terpenoids, steroids, amino acids, carbohydrate, alkaloids and castor showed terpenoids, steroids, carbohydrates, alkaloids and saponins.

The aqueous extract has a good antibacterial activity against Staphylococcus aureus and the inhibitory percentage for papaya and castor are 79.9% and 85% respectively with the maximum concentration used in this.

The anti-inflammatory action is done by HRBC Membrane Stabilization Assay and papaya and castor seed extract showed 56% and 46% inhibition with the maximum concentration used in this. Thus the seeds can be suggested us the preventive agents in diseases and conditions like cancer, edema, tumour, diabetics, anti-viral, cardiovascular diseases, neuro- degenerative diseases to certain extent.

7. Conclusions

The Plants are rich in a wide variety of secondary metabolites, such as tannins, terpenoids, alkaloids, and flavonoids, which have been found to have antimicrobial properties. Phytochemical studies have shown *Carica papaya* to contain alkaloids, carpain, nicotine, flavanols, tannins, and teprenones as well as enzymes such as papain and chymopapain. The black seeds of the papaya are edible and have a sharp, spicy taste. They are sometimes ground and used as a substitute for black pepper. However the seeds seem to have more potent medicinal values than the flesh.

Our studies in this project also indicates that the presence of phytochemical in both castor and seed extract so as it indicate an alternative source of the phytochemical to the body in natural method itself and too it is very cheap. In the study for antimicrobial activity it shows a steady increase in the inhibition with the increase in concentration of seed extract of both castor and papaya seeds. For the anti-inflammatory activity test also shows a relevant inhibitory action against the culture (*S. aureus*) which we are used with the increasing concentration of extract. There by we can suggest that even with a high concentration it may show 100% activity.

8. Future perspective

The studies can be extended for different other organisms too. So that we can cure the diseases to certain extend by using natural products which makes our body quite fresh and make the body devoid of any other unwanted chemicals which are being produced during the consumption of unnatural products. So go natural maximum and keep the nature safe for the future generation also.

References

Adeneye, A. A., & Olagunju, J. A. (2009). Preliminary hypoglycemic and hypolipidemic activities of the aqueous seed extract of *Carica papaya* Linn in Wistar rats. Biol Med, 1(1), 1-10.

Anibijuwon, I. I., & Udeze, A. O. (2009). Antimicrobial activity of *Carica papaya* (pawpaw leaf) on some pathogenic organisms of clinical origin from South-Western Nigeria. *Ethnobotanical Leaflets*, (7), 4.

Anuar, N. S., Zahari, S. S., Taib, I. A., & Rahman, M. T. (2008). Effect of green and ripe *Carica papaya* epicarp extracts on wound healing and during pregnancy. *Food and Chemical Toxicology*, 46(7), 2384-2389.

Anuar, N. S., Zahari, S. S., Taib, I. A., & Rahman, M. T. (2008). Effect of green and ripe Carica papaya epicarp extracts on wound healing and during pregnancy. *Food and Chemical Toxicology*, 46(7), 2384-2389.

Chippada, S. C., Volluri, S. S., Bammidi, S. R., & Vangalapati, M. (2011). In vitro anti-inflammatory activity of methanolic extract of *Centella asiatica* by HRBC membrane stabilisation. Rasayan J Chem, 4(2), 457-60.

Emeruwa, A. C. (1982). Antibacterial substance from *Carica papaya* fruit extract. *Journal of Natural Products*, 45(2), 123-127.

Ezike, A. C., Akah, P. A., Okoli, C. O., Ezeuchenne, N. A., & Ezeugwu, S. (2009). *Carica papaya* (Paw-Paw) unripe fruit may be beneficial in ulcer. *Journal of Medicinal Food*, 12(6), 1268-1273.

Golan, R., Zehavi, U., Naim, M., Patchornik, A., Smirnoff, P., & Herchman, M. (2000). Inhibition of Papaya latex Papain by Photosensitive Inhibitors. 1-(4, 5-Dimethoxy-2-nitrophenyl)-2-nitroethene and 1, 1-Dicyano-2-(4, 5-dimethoxy-2-nitrophenyl)-ethene. *Journal of Protein Chemistry*, 19(2), 117-123.

Ilavarasan, R., Mallika, M., & Venkataraman, S. (2006). Anti-inflammatory and free radical scavenging activity of *Ricinus communis* root extract. *Journal of Ethnopharmacology*, 103(3), 478-480.

Jena, J., & Gupta, A. K. (2012). *Ricinus communis* Linn: a phytopharmacological review. *International Journal of Pharmaceutical Science*, 4(4), 25-29.

Krishnakumar, K. N., Rao, G. P. & Gopakumar, C. S. (2009). Rainfall trends in twentieth century over Kerala, India. *Atmospheric Environment*, 43(11), 1940-1944.

Mandal, S. (2010). Exploration of larvicidal and adult emergence inhibition activities of *Ricinus communis* seed extract against three potential mosquito vectors in Kolkata, India. *Asian Pacific Journal of Tropical Medicine*, 3(8), 605-609.

Puangsri, T., Abdulkarim, S. M., & Ghazali, H. M. (2005). Properties of *Carica papaya* L.(papaya) seed oil following extractions using solvent and aqueous enzymatic methods. *Journal of Food Lipids*, 12(1), 62-76.

Rana, M., Dhamija, H., Prashar, B., & Sharma, S. (2012). *Ricinus communis* L.-a review. *International Journal of PharmTech Research*, 4(4), 1706-1711.

Scarpa, A., & Guerci, A. (1982). Various uses of the castor oil plant (*Ricinus communis* L.) a review. *Journal of Ethnopharmacology*, 5(2), 117-137.

Vij, T., & Prashar, Y. (2015). A review on medicinal properties of *Carica papaya* Linn. *Asian Pacific Journal of Tropical Disease*, 5(1), 1-6.

Yogiraj, V., Goyal, P. K., Chauhan, C. S., Goyal, A., & Vyas, B. (2014). *Carica papaya* Linn: an overview. *International Journal of Herbal Medicine*, 2(5), 01-08.

Appendix

MEDIA COMPOSITION

Nutrient agar

Peptone	: 0.5g
Sodium chloride	: 0.8g
Beef extract	: 0.15g
Yeast extract	: 0.15g
Agar	: 1.5g
Distilled water	: 100ml
pH	: 7.4 ± 0.2

MacConkey agar

Peptic digest of animal tissue	: 20g
Lactose	: 10g
Sodium tourocholate	: 5g
Neutral red	: 0.04g
Agar	: 20g
Distilled water	: 1000ml

MR-VP medium

Glucose phosphate medium

Peptone	: 5g
K_2HPO_4	: 5g
Distilled water	: 1000ml
pH	: 7.4 ± 0.2

Sugar fermentation media

Peptone	: 5g
Sodium chloride	: 20g
0.2% bromocresol purple	: 2.5g
Distilled water	: 1000ml

Tryptone broth

Tryptone	: 10g
Sodium chloride	: 5g
Distilled water	: 1000ml

pH	: 6.8 ± 0.2

Blood agar base

Protease Peptone	: 15g
Liver extract	: 2.5g
Yeast extract	: 5g
NaCl	: 5g
Agar	: 15g
Distilled water	: 1000ml
pH	: 7.4 ± 0.2

Christensen's urea agar

Peptone	: 1g
Dextrose	: 1g
NaCl	: 5g
Monopotassium phosphate	: 2g
Agar	: 0.12g
Phenol red	: 15g
pH	: 6.8 ± 0.2

Simmons citrate agar

Sodium citrate	: 2g
NaCl	: 5g
K_2HPO_4	: 1g
$NH_4H_2PO_4$	: 1g
$MgSO_4$	: 0.2g
Bromothymol blue	: 0.08g
Agar	: 15.5g
Distilled water	: 1000ml
pH	: 6.8 ± 0.2

Triple sugar iron agar test

Peptone	: 10g
Yeast extract	: 3g
Beef extract	: 3g
Lactose	: 10g

Sucrose	: 10g
Dextrose	: 1g
Casein enzyme hydrolysate	: 10g
Sodium chloride	0.5g
Ferrous sulphate	: 0.2g
Sodium thiosulphate	: 0.3g
Phenol red	: 0.024g
Agar	: 12g
Distilled water	: 1000ml
pH	: 7.4 ± 0.2

Muller Hinton agar

Beef extract	: 30g
Casein hydrolysate	: 17.5g
Starch	: 1.5g
Distilled water	: 100ml
Agar	: 15g
pH	: 7.5 ± 0.2

Staining solutions

Gram staining

Crystal violet

Crystal violet	: 10g
100% ethanol	: 100ml
Distilled water	: 900ml

Gram's iodine

Iodine crystals	: 2g
Potassium iodide	: 1g
Distilled water	: 200ml

Safranin

Safranin	: 1g
Ethyl alcohol	: 40ml
Distilled water	: 300ml
pH	: 6.9 ± 0.2

Indicator solutions

Methyl red indicator

Methyl red	: 0.1g
Ethanol	: 300ml
Distilled water	: 100ml

Kovac's reagent

Butanol	: 150ml
p-dimethylaminobenzaldehyde	: 10g
Concentrated HCl	: 15ml

Oxidase reagent

Tetramethyl p-phenylenediaminedihydrochloride	: 0.1g
Distilled water	: 10ml

Voges-Proskauer reagent

Solution A	: 5% w/v solution
α-napthol	: 5g
Alcohol	: 100ml
Solution B	: 4% w/v solution
KOH	: 40g
Distilled water	: 100ml